YOSEMITE
NATIONAL PARK

A
PERSONAL DISCOVERY
BY
ARDETH HUNTINGTON

SIERRA PRESS
MARIPOSA, CA

ACKNOWLEDGMENTS:

"The real voyage of discovery consists not in seeking out new landscapes, but in having new eyes."
—Marcel Proust

I give thanks to the late Yosemite naturalist, Dr. Carl Sharsmith, for giving me "new eyes," and for the friendship of my Sierra-loving friends everywhere. My special appreciation to Dodie, computer Guru on 24-hour call, and to Sharon, Lois, and Jayne—special friends for special reasons.
—A.H.

INSIDE FRONT COVER:
Merced River and Yosemite Valley seen from Gates of the Valley. PHOTO © STEVE MOHLENCAMP
TITLE PAGE:
Half Dome reflected in the calm Merced River. PHOTO © JIM WILSON
THIS PAGE (BELOW):
Mule deer buck at sunset, Yosemite Valley. PHOTO © MICHAEL FRYE
THIS PAGE (RIGHT):
Merced River and glacially sculpted cliffs, autumn afternoon. PHOTO © PAUL MULLINS
PAGE 6/7:
Tuolumne Meadows, sunset. PHOTO © JEFF NICHOLAS
PAGE 7:
Snow hummocks on the banks of the Merced River, mid-winter. PHOTO © JEFF NICHOLAS
BACK COVER (INSET):
Bracken fern and cone. PHOTO © JIM WILSON

4

CONTENTS

PARK OVERVIEW:

Mount Conness, late-afternoon.   PHOTO © GARY MOON

Yosemite—the word evokes a kaleidoscopic mixture of memories: sleeping on moonlit granite the night before visiting the Mount Conness glacier, the fascination of exfoliating granite domes, meadows flowering exquisitely between the Merced Lake and Vogelsang High Sierra Camps, the aroma of pine needles on a hot summer day. To some Yosemite is a playground, to others a revered paradise. It inspires passion—and invites controversy. In trying to capture its essence, writers have glorified it with grandiloquence; praising its *majestic grandeur, infinite lavishness, splendored magnificence;* describing it as *awesome, divine, stunning,* and *sublime.*

In my relationship with Yosemite, I admit to a deep affection. I have expectations of reaffirming those feelings today as I set out for a rendezvous with the full moon at Sentinel Dome. The *scrunch* of my Vibram soles digging into the sandy trail is purposeful, reassuring. Each step increases my anticipation, especially as I near the base of the dome. Sentinel Dome, at 8,122 feet, is not the highest point on the rim of Yosemite Valley (Half Dome exceeds it) but it is my choice for enjoying a "top of the world" feeling on this June day. Its 360-degree view offers one big gulp of Yosemite, a blend of vastness and intimacy. Tonight I hope to recapture the sense of personal discovery I experienced on this dome many years ago.

Occasionally, the word *discovery* suggests historic names, dates, and events. For instance, we say the Mariposa Battalion—when they were sent by the Governor of California to capture Indians allegedly preying on prospectors in the Sierra foothills—"discovered" Yosemite Valley in 1851. What they discovered, however, had already been occupied by Native Americans for thousands of years before the mounted soldiers of the Battalion arrived. I wonder when they discovered it? On the other hand, *discovery* may also be an intensely personal event. Dr. Theodore F. Bunnell, a member of the Mariposa Battalion, recording the event in his book, *The Discovery of Yosemite*, noted that as the vision of waterfalls, domes, and seemingly mile-high cliffs of Yosemite Valley suddenly came into view, he was inexplicably moved, "Tears came to my eyes," he said.

A first look at Yosemite Valley can do that to you. Similar emotions have been described by other chroniclers—John Muir's writings reflect unabashed passion. Ansel Adams said, "When I first saw Yosemite, I knew I had discovered my destiny."

I move steadily along the trail, relishing the rhythm of a hiker's pace, the *caws* of Clark's nutcrackers, the murmur of pine boughs bending to the wind. Suddenly, the dome is ahead of me. It always appears deceptively high, but Sentinel Dome is easily accessed—it's only a mile-and-a-half walk from Glacier Point Road. The trail ascends gradually, turning to the right near the base of the dome, revealing a short scramble up a slope of bedrock slabs leading to the summit. Of all the Yosemite domes that beckon to hikers, Sentinel Dome is second only to Half Dome in popularity. I am surprised to find myself alone on the trail on this perfect summer day.

One last step up and the world above Yosemite Valley comes into view on all sides—a panorama of ridges, valleys, and peaks. El Capitan and Half Dome stand out as the most familiar landmarks. Yosemite Creek slides over a granite lip to create Upper Yosemite Fall, descending quietly—no roar, no thunder—into the shadowy valley below. West of Half Dome are the bald curves of Basket Dome and North Dome. Behind North Dome, Mt. Hoffman's bulk marks the geographic center of Yosemite. To the east, behind Mt. Starr King, stretches the rugged Clark Range. Yosemite Valley is hidden in the chasm between the north and south rims. Fortunately, the artifacts of civilization—stores, hotels, garages, roads, and parking lots—are barely visible in the valley, 3,000 feet below.

Although I share the summit with a dozen others I sit apart, content in my solitude. At my feet, decomposed granite and moisture have created a small garden where Indian paintbrush, mountain pride, and phlox have rooted and bloomed. Sunset richly colors the petals of a nearby penstemon. I watch the distant peaks as they shade from pink to purple. It reassures me to see that the lone Jeffrey pine, photographed by Ansel Adams against a

Dogwood and the Merced River, Spring.

rising moon, is still rooted in granite—no longer living, but now immortal.

As I watch the transition from day to evening, I know that I have found on Sentinel Dome what I sought here: the re-creation of my sense of personal discovery. I have also been able to put aside, for a while at least, the fears I have for this park and its ability to withstand our human impact.

I take one last look at the Jeffrey pine. Its branches appear to reach toward the sliver of light creeping silently from behind Mount Clark—another month, another rising moon. I am reminded of John Muir's words,

> *"We watch and await the reappearance*
> *of everything that melts and fades and dies...*
> *...feeling sure that its next appearance*
> *will be better and*
> *more beautiful than the last."*

Weatherbeaten Jeffrey pine atop Sentinel Dome.

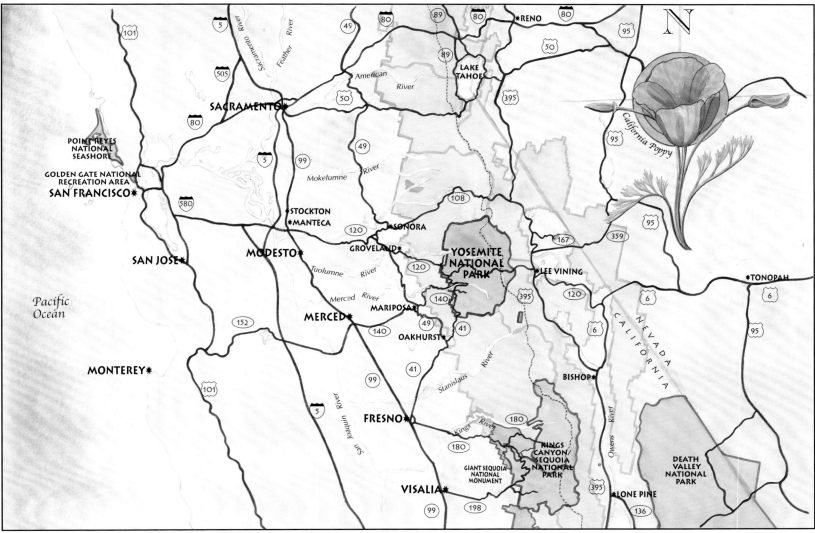

ILLUSTRATION BY DARLECE CLEVELAND

The Sierra Nevada stretches for 400 miles along the length of eastern California, with Yosemite National Park in the very heart of it. The eastern edge of the Sierra forms a dramatic escarpment as it descends to the basin and range topography of Nevada. To the west, the landscape slopes gently for 56 miles to the foothills above California's Central Valley. Along the Sierra crest, within Yosemite's boundaries, peaks rise up to 13,000 feet, surrounded by dozens of lakes—1,169 square miles of entrancing mountain scenery.

Yosemite can be reached by highways from the north, south, east, and west. Greyhound and AMTRAK provide connections from Merced and additional bus service by YARTS (Yosemite Area Regional Transportation System) is available. Arriving in such comfort leads one to admire the adventurous souls who, a hundred years ago, rode horses and mules over rough wagon roads for many days in order to enjoy Yosemite's "scenes of wonder and curiosity." These same scenes are easily reached today via well-graded highways that trace the mountains' contours.

Highway 140, called the All Year Highway because it is at an elevation that usually escapes heavy winter snowfall, winds through the Merced River Canyon as it approaches the park. From March-into-April the hillsides above the river are painted orange with poppies and redbud is in bloom along the roadsides. At Arch Rock Entrance Station the road passes between two tall slabs of leaning granite, then heads upriver into Yosemite Valley.

Highway 120 comes from the San Francisco Bay Area and the "gold-country" of the Sierra foothills, curving through pine forests that occasionally open enough to provide glimpses of the Tuolumne River. Ten miles after entering the park is the junction with Tioga Road, which leads east to the high country of Tuolumne Meadows and Tioga Pass.

Highway 41, south of Yosemite, heads north from Fresno, ascends the foothills to Oakhurst, then takes you through a fragrant Ponderosa pine forest to the South Entrance. Just inside this entrance, at the end of a 2-mile spur road, is the Mariposa Grove of Giant Sequoias.

Tioga Road (Highway 120) is seasonal. Snow usually closes the road from early-November until at least late-May. From Mono Lake and Highway 395 to the east, the road climbs in sweeping curves to Tioga Pass, Yosemite's highest entry at 9,941 feet, accompanied by stunning alpine scenery all along the way.

PAGE 12 & 13: Relflections in Upper Young Lake, early morning. PHOTO © CHARLES CRAMER

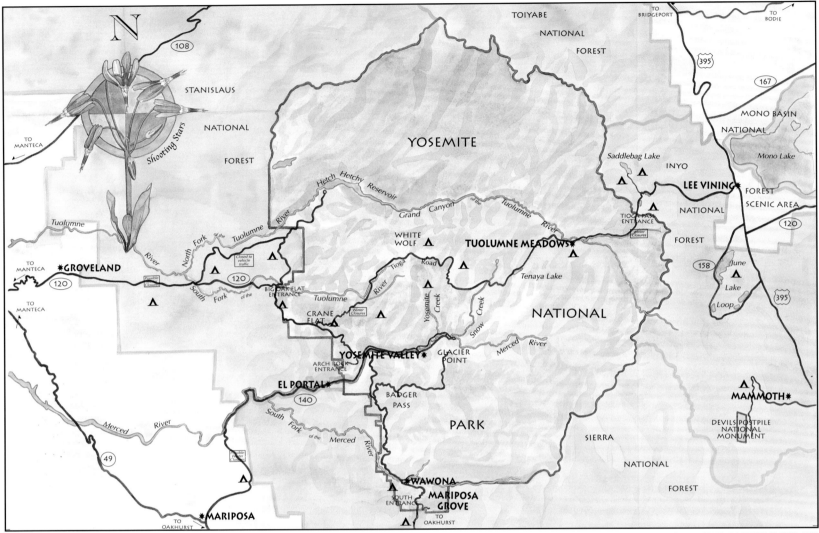

ILLUSTRATION BY DARLECE CLEVELAND

Yosemite National Park is large, roughly the size of Rhode Island. About 94% of the park is classified as wilderness, accessible by trails only, but it is possible to drive to six major areas of sightseeing, including the heart of the park—Yosemite Valley. Each area offers something unique, and all are noted for superb sightseeing and hiking. Driving time between destinations can be one to several hours, not including sightseeing stops. *The Yosemite Road Guide* is a book available for purchase that gives descriptions of viewpoints and historic spots keyed to roadside markers. A guided-tour audio tape may also enhance the enjoyment of driving.

The descriptions below can't begin to detail the wealth of recreation, hiking, and historical explorations to be found in these areas. See *The Yosemite Guide* for full explanations of seasonal activities and services. This newspaper and a park map are free with your entrance fee—which is valid for 7 days.

Yosemite Valley is everyone's number one stop and all highways lead to Yosemite Valley's west-end, where sightseeing begins. The glacially sculpted walls of the valley offer some of the most spectacular scenery in the world. Yosemite Falls, El Capitan, and Half Dome are among the most famous features.

Mariposa Grove is home to nearly 500 giant sequoias—including The Fallen Monarch and Grizzly Giant. Winding paths invite you to stroll among the Big Trees for close views of these amazing trees, or a tram ride may be purchased. Wawona is known for the Wawona Hotel, Pioneer Yosemite History Center, fine hiking, and serenity.

Glacier Point, on Yosemite Valley's south rim, provides awesome vistas of the extraordinary Clark Range and reveals all of Yosemite Valley. Hiking trails in this area lead to Taft Point and Sentinel Dome, and to Yosemite Valley via the Panorama and Four-Mile Trails.

Crane Flat is a pleasant forest and meadow region on the park's western edge. It is 2 miles from the Tuolumne Grove of Giant Sequoias, where 25 huge trees of the same species found in Mariposa Grove are sheltered.

Tioga Road ranges in elevation from 6,200 feet at Crane Flat to 9,941 feet at Tioga Pass. Along the route are lakes, peaks, and domes of outstanding beauty. Tuolumne Meadows, 8 miles west of Tioga Pass, is known as the hub for wilderness trips into the High Sierra.

Hetch Hetchy provides access to the park's northern wilderness and is known for O'Shaughnessy Dam and reservoir, as well as for its springtime waterfall displays.

OPPOSITE: The view from Mount Hoffman—the geographic center of Yosemite—late afternoon. PHOTO © GEORGE WUERTHNER

YOSEMITE VALLEY:

Bridalveil Fall, sunset.   PHOTO © MICHAEL FRYE

"...then I walked down to the ledge and crawled out upon the overhanging rocks. In all my life I think I shall see nothing else so grand, so sublime, so beautiful—beauty of a beauty not of this earth—as that vision of the Valley."

The emotions expressed in 1851, by soldiers of the Mariposa Battalion, the first non-natives to enter Yosemite Valley, can be understood by today's visitors as they gaze into "the incomparable Valley" from Tunnel View. Overwhelmed by this vision, most visitors no longer have any doubt as to the reason for Yosemite Valley's fame. It is seven square-miles of exquisite scenery: waterfalls leap from 3,000-foot rims and glacially carved walls are crowned with domes and arches. The valley's most distinctive features, El Capitan and Half Dome, are recognized by visitors from all over the world.

All park roads lead to Yosemite Valley. Entering from the south, on Highway 41, you will be awed by the panorama at Tunnel View; approaching from other highways you will be enchanted by the drive between Pohono Bridge and Bridalveil Fall in the valley's west end. This drive is appealing in every season: a show of dogwood blossoms in the spring, the golden blaze of big-leaf maple and oaks in the fall, and in winter, snow outlining branches and twigs and laying pillows on lowering pine boughs.

Viewed from Glacier Point the valley appears deceptively spacious with generous expanses of meadow. Looking up from any place on the valley floor, however, you are immediately aware of the depth and closeness of the walls. The predominant granite formations along the south wall of the valley are Cathedral Rocks, Cathedral Spires, Sentinel Rock, and Glacier Point. On the north wall are El Capitan, Three Brothers, Lost Arrow, Royal Arches, North Dome, and Washington Column. When viewing them from the valley floor they can be seen most distinctly from a distance, from the opposite side of the Merced River, or from across a meadow rather than from a neck-craning perspective.

The size of Yosemite Valley, relative to the park as a whole, has always been misleading. The valley measures just 7 square miles,

which makes it only a small part of the entire 1,169-square-mile park. South Side Drive enters the Valley from the west. The road passes a turnout for viewing Bridalveil Fall and El Capitan, which looms into view across the river, startling in its immensity. The road follows the Merced River through a forested area of Ponderosa pine and incense cedar until suddenly you are in the midst of the first of the valley's several large meadows. It is a dramatic moment. To the left, Yosemite Falls plunges over the rim of the north wall in two huge leaps, divided by a stretch of cascades. A stroll across the meadow on the boardwalk is a satisfying way to contemplate the view. The configuration of the valley is not straight, but sinuous. The road leaves this first meadow and winds almost imperceptibly to the right, bordered again by pines interspersed with house-sized erratics—granite boulders deposited here by glaciers. At the extreme east end of the valley stands its monolithic overseer—Half Dome.

There is no single ideal way to explore Yosemite Valley. Open-air touring trams are an option and shuttle buses will transport you to Lower Yosemite Falls, the Mirror Lake Meadow trailhead, and Happy Isles. Perhaps the most satisfaction, if you have the time, is to walk away from the mainstream of visitation—into the woods or along the river—and experience the beauty from a perspective of solitude. Contemplation was a pastime urged by Yosemite naturalist Carl Sharsmith. "Look around you," he said, "and see that the world of little things can be as beguiling as the large. First you learn the names of the waterfalls, then the granite. Soon you ask, 'Is that a Ponderosa pine or a Jeffrey?' You want to know the names of the oaks, the birds, the flowers. Finally, even the smallest things become fascinating."

In spite of its reputation as a magnet that attracts millions of people every year, it is possible to find solitude in the valley. Considering the geographic limitations of the valley, annual visitation in the millions is a disturbing statistic. The impact on this limited locale, the "human footprint" as it is called, has left Yosemite Valley vulnerable to becoming despoiled. For years park managers have struggled with the dilemma of balancing preserva-

Yosemite Valley as seen from Tunnel View, spring afternoon.

tion and use.

Although a visit to Yosemite Valley brings pleasure to millions, development, crowding, and congestion have had a noticeable impact. Responses by park management to these conditions have been encouraging. Recent changes to the Valley Management Plan include closing the east-end to private vehicles, establishing one-way roads, reassigning parking lots, encouraging sightseeing on foot and bicycle, establishing a free valley shuttle bus system, and supporting alternative transportation systems from outside the park. Plans are being laid for even broader prospects for improvement, an ongoing aspect of the concern for Yosemite Valley's future. Because it involves input from a public whose feelings for Yosemite Valley are strong, often pulling in contradictory directions, achieving a Valley Plan that will favorably affect the quality of a visitor's experience, yet be balanced with ecosystem protection and restoration objectives, will always be a challenge.

Black oaks in Yosemite Valley, autumn morning.

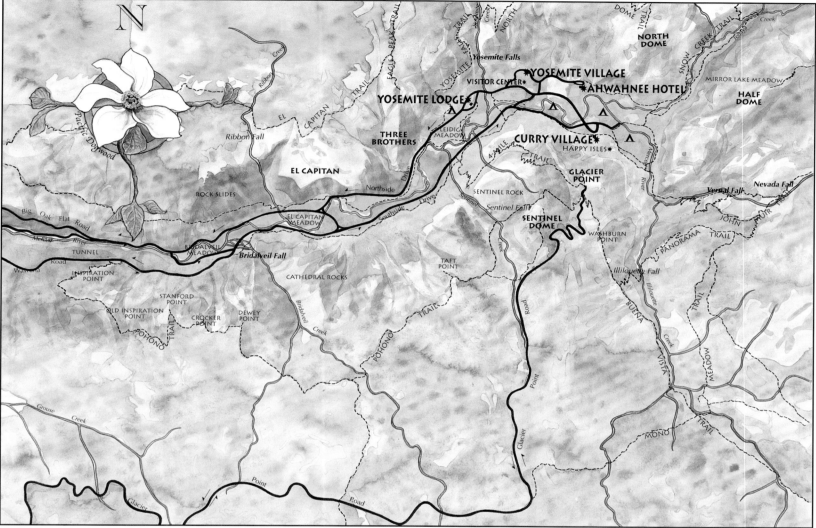

ILLUSTRATION BY DARLECE CLEVELAND

All roads entering Yosemite Valley merge near the Bridalveil Fall parking lot. There, they become a one-way road that extends almost the full length of the valley's south side, crosses the Merced River, and heads back along the river's north side.

After parking your car (follow signs to parking lots) begin your exploration of the Valley floor with a visit to the Visitor Center, which offers geology exhibits and an informative film that explains park history and attractions. Books, maps, brochures, and trail guides are available for sale from the Yosemite Association Bookstore. Park Rangers are also on hand to answer questions.

It is wise to keep your copy of *The Yosemite Guide* with you when touring the park, but especially Yosemite Valley. It is provided free of charge, along with the official park map, at entrance stations. The *Guide* contains all pertinent park information including daily events and activities for all regions, a Yosemite Valley hiking guide, a park sightseeing map, and, most important, a map of the Valley's free shuttle bus system.

Touring Yosemite Valley is made easier by parking your vehicle and using the free shuttle bus system. Shuttle buses are the most convenient way to get around the valley. They run on a frequent schedule, including evenings, stopping at popular destinations such as the Visitor Center, lodgings, campgrounds, seasonal recreation centers (ice rink, river rafting, stables), and bicycle rentals. Shuttle buses are designed as transportation and are not considered sightseeing buses, although bus drivers sometimes add generalized sightseeing information to their announcements. Hikers can use shuttle buses to get to and from major valley trailheads, such as the John Muir Trail (Vernal Fall, Nevada Fall, and Half Dome, plus wilderness destinations), and to the Upper Yosemite Falls Trail. Easy day hikes (Mirror Lake Meadow and some points along the Valley Loop Trail) are easily accessed by shuttle buses.

Yosemite Village, in the valley's east-end, is the commercial hub of the valley. Here you will find the Visitor Center, Indian Village, museums, Pioneer Cemetery, post office, Ansel Adams Gallery, Wilderness Center (summer only), Degnan's Deli, Village Store, Art Activity Center (seasonal), ATM, and certain administrative offices.

Curry Village is a lodging complex, also in the east-end of the valley, with cabins, tent-cabins, food service, mountain shop, amphitheater for evening programs, and shower facilities. It is about a 1-mile walk from Yosemite Village.

PAGE 20 & 21: Early morning fog and clouds shroud El Capitan, winter morning. PHOTO © RUSS BISHOP

President Teddy Roosevelt (l.) and John Muir (r.) at Glacier Point (Upper Yosemite Fall in background). PHOTO COURTESY NPS, YOSEMITE COLLECTION

JOHN MUIR

John Muir is regarded as the most passionate defender of Yosemite from those who would exploit it for personal profit. In a life filled with accomplishments, his major achievement was leading the successful crusade for federal management of parts of Yosemite in danger of being despoiled by manipulation and exploitation. Mainly through his efforts, Yosemite National Park came into being in 1890.

Muir was born in Scotland in 1838, to a family that soon emigrated to a Wisconsin farm. Rural life for John was harsh, particularly under a tyrannical father who ruled with rod and religion. As a young man neither a job nor university classes satisfied him (although he was successful at both), so he chose to travel, seeking what he called "the freedom of wild places." His wanderings eventually led him to Yosemite Valley, where he gloried in its magnificence and in his leisure to explore. He scrutinized every aspect of Nature and kept detailed journals of his feelings, experiences, and discoveries. Geology classes at the University of Wisconsin had given him a background in experiential glacial research that led to his theory on the formation of Yosemite Valley, namely, that it was not created by cataclysmic events, but by the force of glacial movement. These theories, though contradicted by eminent geologist Josiah D. Whitney, were ultimately proven to be valid.

Considerable as Muir's contributions to science were, even greater was his stature in defining and defending the principles of conservation. An eloquent speaker and writer, he was effective in lobbying legislators to eliminate rampant exploitation of Yosemite's fragile beauty. His arguments convinced President Teddy Roosevelt to support conservationist's plans to unify The Yosemite Grant with Yosemite National Park.

Muir married, raised a family, and achieved financial success as overseer of his father-in-law's fruit ranches in Martinez, California. He also had opportunities to travel world-wide, championing his convictions for the necessity of preserving public lands. His final struggle was undoubtedly his toughest, the legislative battle to save Yosemite's Hetch Hetchy Valley from being inundated by the damming of the Tuolumne River to provide water for the City of San Francisco. Muir was devastated when the Raker Act, approving the dam, passed Congress in 1913. He died on Christmas Eve in 1914, worn out, they say, by his efforts and saddened by defeat. His spirit lives in the impassioned prose of his books and in his legacy—the creation of Yosemite National Park.

Ponderosa pines frame the Ahwahnee Hotel.

THE AHWAHNEE HOTEL

Today, the idea of building a luxury hotel within a national park may be unsettling to some, but it is hard to deny the magnificence of the "massive and memorable" Ahwahnee Hotel. Built in the 1920s, the Ahwahnee's six-stories of stone-and-timber is worthy of its setting and is now listed on the National Register of Historic Places.

The hotel was conceived in 1925, when the newest park concessionaire, the Yosemite Park and Curry Company, began to feel its influence during the presidency of Dr. Donald Tressider. The 33-year old Stanford alumnus, a creative promoter, had firm convictions about the need for a first-class Yosemite hotel, and Steven P. Mather, Director of the National Park Service, encouraged and supported Tressider's plans. A budget of $600,000 was approved for a hotel with 100-bedrooms-with-baths, a tasteful lobby, and a gourmet kitchen that could serve a dining room seating 500. Gilbert Stanley Underwood (who also designed Grand Canyon Lodge and lodges at Bryce and Zion National Parks) was hired as architect and Tressider added ideas along the way.

A Yosemite Valley site with spectacular views of Glacier Point, Yosemite Falls, and Half Dome was selected for the hotel. Occupied at the time by the Coffman and Kenney Stables—whose business had deteriorated since automobiles had become the preferred mode of transportation—the park service had the stables razed and, later, moved nearby Camp 8—according to historian Shirley Sargent, so that campers and hotel guests "would not conflict." Construction began in 1926, and, after numerous design conflicts, the hotel was finally completed a year later—commemorated by both a public ceremony and an elegant private party.

All guests—including a celebrity clientele of queens, kings, presidents, and film stars—are impressed by the Ahwahnee's beauty. The Great Lounge, of monumental proportions, includes fireplaces large enough for a person to stand within and ten stained-glass, floor-to-ceiling, windows intricately inlaid with symbolic motifs. The Dining Room, also of awesome size, boasts a 34-foot-high trestle-and-beam ceiling and majestic windows. It is an appropriate stage for the Bracebridge Dinner held annually in December. Although still the most expensive lodgings in Yosemite, the original appeal of The Ahwahnee has evolved over the years. Today, the Great Lounge is made lively by family conviviality at tea-time, and the elegant dining room welcomes all park visitors; many choose to enjoy the elaborate Sunday Brunch.

Upper Yosemite Fall, foggy spring morning.

PHOTO © JEFF GRANDY

WATERFALLS OF YOSEMITE

One glorious waterfall would bring prestige to any national park. Yosemite Valley boasts a bonanza: five major falls and numerous minor falls—worthy of attention during their brief life in early-spring but not lasting into summer. Countless ephemerals flow for a brief period, splashing across valley walls during the first warm weeks of May, then disappearing from the scene.

Yosemite's waterfalls are at their peak during the months of April, May, and June when 75% of the annual snowmelt occurs. May is usually when they are at their best. By July, most surface water is gone and certain falls either dry up or are diminished. Some falls remain flowing because they aren't dependent on snowmelt, but are fed by watersheds that hold more water, for a longer time.

One park visitor commented, "Watching falling water is as mesmerizing as staring into the flames of a campfire." Yosemite Valley's five major falls fascinate today as they always have, both for gazing and picture-taking. Bridalveil Fall, Upper and Lower Yosemite Falls, and the two "giant staircase" falls of the Merced River—Nevada Fall and Vernal Fall—are among the most photographed scenes in the park.

Bridalveil and Yosemite Falls were formed as granite-crushing glacial ice moved relentlessly along the course of the Merced River, isolating tributary streams from their mainstream connection so that they dropped directly into the newly created valley below. Nevada and Vernal Falls are the result of glaciers moving across unjointed granite that did not fracture, but was cut into huge blocks of differing elevations, forming a "staircase" effect. Deep in its gorge at the southeastern-end of Yosemite Valley is Illilouette Fall, not visible from the valley floor, but a reward for hikers who choose the Panorama Trail.

Ribbon Fall, the highest single leap in North America, drops a spectacular 1,600 feet in its recessed gorge west of El Capitan. "Ribbon" aptly describes this slender shaft, which diminishes to a scant trickle by late-June. In spring, The Cascades provide a display of dashing, leaping water. Formed by two creeks, Tamarack and Cascade, they plunge down the crevassed north wall of the Merced River gorge, west of Yosemite Valley. They can be seen from a turnout on Highway 140.

Examples of ephemeral falls include Horsetail Fall on El Capitan's east wall and Staircase Fall below Glacier Point.

OPPOSITE: Ephemeral Horsetail Fall, on the east face of El Capitan. PHOTO © MICHAEL FRYE

TUOLUMNE MEADOWS & TIOGA ROAD:

Half Dome seen from Olmsted Point, sunset.　　PHOTO © JIM WILSON

Tuolumne Meadows is considered the hub of the Yosemite's high country. Located on Tioga Road, 8 miles west of Tioga Pass, it is about an hour-and-a-half drive from Yosemite Valley and 45 minutes from Crane Flat. Here you will find one of the most admired settings in Yosemite's high country, a basin about 2-1/2 miles long and a half mile wide, described as the largest sub-alpine meadow system in the High Sierra. These expansive meadows are graced by the Tuolumne River—whose Dana and Lyell Forks flow from their respective peaks. Their waters co-mingle alongside the John Muir Trail where they cascade among rocks to become a placid meander at the meadow's edge.

Tuolumne Meadows has an extremely short growing season because of its 8,600-foot elevation. The greening of the meadows does not begin until early July and doesn't last long. "People are disappointed in the brownish appearance of the meadows from late July on," says ranger-naturalist Bob Fry. "The fading coloration can be understood when you consider the rapidity with which the short-haired sedges grow up, seed, and settle back into dormancy—all within 6 weeks."

Tuolumne Meadows is known for its stunningly picturesque scenery, but is also rich in geologic and human history, has a genial summer climate, and features easy and challenging trails heading in all directions. You can stay in a campground or in a tent-cabin at Tuolumne Meadows Lodge, climb a dome, enjoy a day-hike, fish, cool off in the river, or sit on a rock and enjoy gazing at the surrounding peaks. You can also take a walk with a ranger to learn something about the region's natural history—although an hour walk could never cover Tuolumne's more than 40 species of birds, 20 mammals, fascinating geology, and abundance of plant species.

When Yosemite National Park was established in 1890, Tuolumne Meadows was an area accessible only by foot or pack animals. Explorers, miners, and sheepherders were its main visitors. John Lembert built a cabin at Soda Springs and lived there as a hermit for 10 years. Lembert Dome, the asymmetric piece of granite called a *rouche moutinee* (sheepback) that dominates the meadow, was named for him. Soda Springs would later become a

private camping spot for Sierra Club members and friends, until the club sold the land to the park service in 1972.

Summer and early autumn are the major seasons for visitation to Tuolumne Meadows—winter's first sizable snowfall usually closes Tioga Road until late-May. However, cross-country skiers with proficient skill may ski through Tioga Pass to enjoy Tuolumne's snowy meadows and trails.

Although a frequent visitor to Yosemite Valley, I first discovered Tuolumne Meadows when I enrolled in a seminar sponsored by the Yosemite Association—a week of day hikes centered on the topic "Sub-Alpine Botany" led by Yosemite's ranger-naturalist Bob Fry. This was not only my introduction to Tuolumne Meadows, but my first experience at entering Yosemite by way of Tioga Pass, and I was unaware of the treat that awaited me.

I left Los Angeles on a Friday evening in a blue VW bug, the hood-space crammed with food (bears were less car-clever in 1980) and a back seat lumpy with sleeping bag, tent, and pillows. Although I was a bit concerned about finding a campsite in the dark after an 8-hour drive, my anticipation of a weekend botany seminar in the sub-alpine high country of Tuolumne Meadows overcame my feelings of nervousness. The sky had changed from blue-violet to black when I turned west from Highway 395 and began the ascent up Lee Vining Canyon toward Tioga Pass. I was alone on the road, paying attention to its twists and turns. The climb was hard on the little car. Suddenly, as I floored the gas pedal to gain the crest at Ellery Lake, the scene changed dramatically. Like a theater in which a technician in the booth had, on cue, turned a spotlight on the stage, the canyon lit up. A rising full moon had slipped into view between two masses of mountain and before me I could now see peaks behind peaks, rock chutes, snow-filled cirques, and the surface of Ellery Lake silvered by moonlight. Unlike Ansel Adams, who jumped onto the roof of his car and took out his camera when he found himself suddenly surprised by the moonrise at Hernandez, New Mexico—I merely pulled the steering wheel to the left and ground to a stop on a gravel pull-out and sat there mesmerized.

OPPOSITE: Mammoth Peak reflected in tarn at Tioga Pass, late afternoon. PHOTO © HOWARD WEAMER

Wildflowers carpeting Tuolumne Meadows.

A dozen seminar participants met in front of the ranger station on Saturday morning. I was nervous, intimidated by the number of experienced botanists present, including two Ph.D's and a woman who had just published a book on edible plants. I, on the other hand, was at the stage of calling flowers "that pink one" or "the one with the fuzzy leaves." We followed Bob in the direction of Soda Springs where wildflowers were plentiful. Suddenly I was the only person standing—everyone, including Bob, was down on hands and knees peering through lenses and mumbling botanical terminology in Latin. My inauspicious beginning had a fine ending, however, because Bob—the consummate understanding teacher—gave this novice lessons in plant identification that night around his campfire.

Between its high-country appeal, the scenery, and the botanical education, one couldn't ask for a finer introduction to Tuolumne Meadows.

The Tuolumne River below Unicorn Peak (left).

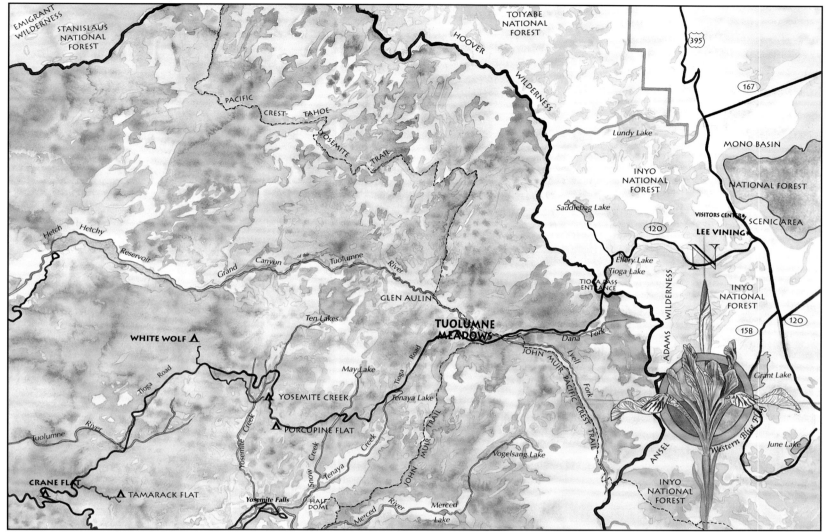

ILLUSTRATION BY DARLECE CLEVELAND

The Mono Trail, mining, and Stephen H. Mather are three reasons why Tioga Road exists today. This modern trans-Sierra route, extending 50 east-west miles, follows the route of the old Mono Trail, a trade route linking Miwok encampments in the region of Yosemite Valley with the Paiutes of the Mono Lake region to the east. This ancient route was first used by explorers and, later, by miners on foot and in wagons as the lure of gold and silver brought prospectors from the used-up western foothill mines to the eastern Sierra.

Mining claims in the Tioga region were the impetus for the Great Sierra Consolidated Silver Company to build a road to bring machinery and supplies from Crocker's Station up and over Tioga Pass to Bennettville, an ambitious undertaking of 56-miles. Work was begun in 1882, and the road reached its destination on September 4, 1883—an incredible achievement that required a major in-vestment of money and men. The profits from the mine turned out to be minimal but the road, although rough and poorly maintained for many years to come, was hailed as a success.

Steven H. Mather was appointed Assistant Director of the Department of Interior in 1915. Enthusiastic about Yosemite's future as a tourist mecca, he looked for ideas that would bring more people to the park. With the popularity of auto-mobile travel increasing, he decided that im-proved roads were the answer and considered buying the privately owned Tioga Road as a way to entice visitors to Yosemite's high country. When he discovered that it was available for purchase for $15,500, he campaigned among his wealthier friends for funds, paid the balance out of his own pocket, then worked out details with Congress to allow the government to accept Tioga Road as his gift to Yosemite National Park.

The Highway 120 Corridor has become a vi-tal part of Yosemite life, its opening eagerly awaited every spring after its winter closure. It is an important connection in several respects: it links the west and east sides of the Sierra with a dependable transportation route, takes people to backcountry trailheads and campgrounds, and allows sightseers to enjoy magnificent Yosemite scenery previously not easily accessible.

Destinations along the route include Crane Flat, the Tuolumne Grove of Big Trees, White Wolf Lodge and campground, Siesta Lake, Yosemite Creek, May Lake Road, Olmsted Point, Tenaya Lake, Tuolumne Meadows, Dana Meadows, and Tioga Pass.

GLACIERS AND GRANITE

James Hutchings was correct when he declared Half Dome (*Tis-sa-ack*) "the greatest attraction of Yosemite Valley," but in proposing that a "convulsion of Nature" robbed the dome of it's other half, he placed himself in erroneous, though eminent, company. Geologist Josiah D. Whitney, a Harvard professor and head of the United States Geological Survey, also decided that it was a cataclysmic event that was responsible for the formation of Yosemite Valley. In one of his more poetic descriptions, he declared, "Half Dome has gone down in the wreck of matter and the crush of worlds."

It was John Muir who first deduced the reality of Yosemite's geologic past: that rivers of glacial ice, thousands of feet thick, thrusting their way through granite over eons of time, had been responsible for creating Yosemite Valley's splendor. Muir's inquisitive ramblings in the High Sierra led him to clues of glacial activity, such as moraines, glacial polish, striations, and erratic boulders. Eventually he found an active glacier on Merced Peak. Whitney continued to scorn Muir's hypothesis, calling him a "mere sheepherder," in reference to Muir's first job in the Sierra Nevada. Today, it is an accepted theory that glaciers were critical in shaping the granitic walls of Yosemite Valley.

Granite dominates the Yosemite area and much of the Sierra Nevada as well. Mount Hoffman, the geographic center of Yosemite National Park, and most of the terrain visible from it, are composed of granite formed deep within the earth by solidification of formerly molten rock, subsequently sculpted by glacial action into the famed formations of Yosemite Valley.

IT TOOK 500 MILLION YEARS

To understand the domes, cliffs, and waterfalls of Yosemite it is necessary to realize that geologic processes have been at work here

for several hundred million years. The succession of processes leading to the Valley's present form are complicated, but can be summarized in six steps: **1.** 50 million years ago the landscape consisted of rolling hills, broad valleys and meandering streams. The Merced River meandered through a shallow trough whose slopes supported hardwood forests. **2.** Ten million years ago, forces in the crust of the earth forced the Sierra Nevada to be uplifted and tilted westward, accelerating the river's flow and causing it to cut deeper in its valley. The climate grew cooler and forests dominated. **3.** Three million years

ago, continuing uplifting action resulted in a landscape of intricate, steep-walled canyons. The Merced gorge was 3,000 feet deep, while it's tributary streams, carrying less volume of water, cut into the land more slowly. The approach of the Ice Age brought a colder climate and thinning forests. **4.** One million to 250,000 years ago several glacial advances filled Yosemite Valley to its brim with ice. Half Dome projected 900 feet above this ice-filled gorge, but many peaks to the north were engulfed. The relentless movement of the ice gouged the valley into a U-shape, and the tributaries of the Merced became cascades. **5.** 30,000 years ago the last glacier advanced into the valley, terminating near El Capitan and Bridalveil Fall. Though smaller than preceding glaciers, it had the power to enlarge the valley even further. **6.** 10,000 years ago the melting glacier created ancient Lake Yosemite, dammed at its west end by the glacier's terminal moraine.

Lakes, no doubt, followed each period of glaciation, formed by glacial recession and subsequent melting. These lake beds, originally incised as much as 2,000 feet into the bedrock, gradually became filled with sediments. The last of Yosemite Valley's "lakes" also filled with sediment, and became the basis for the flat valley floor that today supports meadows and forests. Mirror Lake is now evolving into a meadow by this same process of sedimentation.

The tremendous power of glaciers is difficult to visualize. Ice flows of tremendous depth and weight crushed and tore away mammoth blocks and slabs of granite, carving out a valley as they moved. However, blocks of granite can only be plucked from rock that is already jointed or fractured. The sheer walls of Upper Yosemite Fall and Half Dome were not carved directly by ice flow, but were pre-formed by vertical joints within

---

ABOVE: Glacial polish and striations on granite dome above Olmsted Point (Tenaya Lake is visible in the distance). PHOTO © DENNIS FLAHERTY

1. Fifty-million years ago

2. Ten-million years ago

3. Three-million years ago

the rock. The glaciers exploited these weaknesses. If massive granite sections contained few joints or fractures a glacier could not force breakage, but only file and polish the contours as it passed—El Capitan is a classic example.

The last period of glaciation reached its maximum extent about 15,000 to 20,000 years ago. Then the earth's climate began to warm and a final glacial recession began. Since the close of the Ice Age, little major change has taken place in Yosemite Valley. The main geologic force at work today on the granite of Yosemite is the non-glacial erosion of freeze-thaw cycles and gravity. Proof of contemporary erosion is seen in the rock materials piled at the base of the cliffs, called talus slopes—the result of walls breaking down due to natural weathering.

HALF DOME'S OTHER HALF
Looking at Half Dome, it is not unreasonable to assume that it once had another half. That is not the case; probably 80% of the monolith is still there. Geologists surmise that a small glacier at the bottom of the dome quarried off a lower section or "sheet" from Half Dome's surface, undermining a narrow upper portion and causing it to drop away. The shedding of a dome's outer sheets, plates, or scales is called exfoliation, or spalling.

DOMES AND EXFOLIATION
Domes on the north side of the valley—North Dome, Basket Dome, and Mt. Watkins—were completely overridden by glaciers, but those to the south—Half Dome, Sentinel Dome and Mt. Starr King—were not. The upper slopes of Half Dome are estimated to be from 3 to 10 million years old and were shaped long before the Ice Age, which suggests exfoliation, not glaciers, as its shaping force.

A process called "load relief" is the dominant cause of exfoliation. A rock that will become a dome is one that has been buried as much as five miles below the surface, under great pressure from overlying materials. As these overlying materials are removed by erosion the rock expands as the pressure is released. During this expansion, its "shells" are cast off, creating a dome—a process often compared to the peeling layers of an onion. Cracks parallel to the newly exposed surfaces eventually allow the surface layers to break away—leaving more curved than sharp angles.

4. One-million to 250,000 years ago

5. 30,000 years ago

6. 10,000 years ago

Black bear.

PHOTO © MICHAEL FRYE

BEARS

It used to be called Yosemite's "bear problem"—the annual property damage amounting to hundreds of thousands of dollars caused by bears in search of campers' and backpackers' food. Now it is labeled, more accurately, "a people problem." After all, the bears are not to blame.

Driven by appetite, curiosity, and a powerful sense of smell, bears explore their Yosemite domain seeking the human food often made accessible to them through careless storage habits. Prowling at all hours, and in every season, some have learned to invade cars, ransack ice chests and backpacks, and examine anything odiferous to locate a meal. Through negligence people suffer a loss of possessions, but the bears suffer a greater loss. Those that forego their fear of humans and become aggressive must be trapped and killed. Relocation is frequently unsuccessful because bears will often return to a familiar habitat and continue their unnatural foraging habits—often more assertively than before.

Black bears (*Ursus americanus*) may be black, brown, or cinnamon-colored. Their habitat is forests below 8,000 feet in elevation—their natural diet an assortment of grasses, insects, acorns, berries, and carrion.

Most spend the winter months in hibernation, emerging occasionally during periods of warm weather. Females (sows) produce litters of 2 to 3 cubs every other year. Its life span can be as great as 25 years.

Unfortunately, the park service has not always been a good teacher of bear protection. In the 1930s, bear feeding was offered as an official evening entertainment. Crowds gathered at the garbage dump next to Curry Village near an illuminated platform on which rangers had piled leftovers from valley restaurant kitchens. The feast satisfied the bears while park visitors clicked cameras and enjoyed this close-up view of Yosemite wildlife. Access to human food, however, eliminated the "wild" from wildlife as bears altered their instinctive feeding habits and taught their young how to be successful by depending on humans for food.

Solving "the people problem" is centered on one theme: don't be bear-careless. Store all food and other scented items properly. Use metal food lockers, backpacker canisters, and bear-resistant refuse bins. Remove food from parked vehicles. Keep a clean camp and a clean car. In the presence of bears, always stay at a distance and never approach or try to feed them.

OPPOSITE: Summer foliage on the shore of Siesta Lake. PHOTO © LARRY ULRICH   **PAGE 36 & 37:** Mount Dana and high country pond, summer. PHOTO © DICK DIETRICH

Smoke from the Arch Rock Fire, 1990.

THE ROLE OF FIRE

Starting without warning and spreading swiftly, forest fires can be devastating—and deadly. But fire is not always a destroyer. Its regenerative powers can be beneficial to plants, animals, and people. Yosemite's Native Americans had respect for natural fires, and they deliberately encouraged slow-spreading fires through forest undergrowth. Historic photographs show Yosemite Valley's mixed conifer forests as more open—free of understory vegetation and ground litter—with meadows far more extensive than they are today.

Until a few decades ago, park management felt that all fires should be suppressed. However, a century of suppressing natural fires allowed forest debris to accumulate in massive fuel loads, such as those that contributed to the catastrophic Yosemite fires of 1990 and 1996. Experience has taught us when to intervene to prevent devastating fires, and why we need intelligent policies of control as well as public education about the role of fire in the park.

More than 95% of Yosemite's fires are started by lightning. Because we now accept lightning fires as a part of Yosemite's natural ecosystem, in some park areas, and under appropriate conditions, lightning caused fires may be allowed to burn. Another acceptable fire is the *prescribed burn*, used in and around Yosemite's developed areas and in areas filled with unnaturally high amounts of dead wood. Visitors will notice smoldering ground along roadsides, when weather conditions are favorable, and see signs announcing: Management Fire—Do Not Report. Intermittently reduced visibility from smoke may partially obscure park vistas and anyone with respiratory problems should use caution when exerting themselves in smoky areas. Fortunately, the long-term benefits of Yosemite's proven Fire Management Program outweigh temporary inconveniences.

The benefits of fire to certain plant species, such as giant sequoias, are well known. The sequoia is dependent on heat for reproduction. Heat opens its cones, releasing seeds, and fire burns away litter on the forest floor. This allows the short, immature roots of new seedlings to reach the nutritious soil layer needed for their growth. Experimental burns in sequoia groves in the 1960s resulted in a marked increase of new seedlings.

OPPOSITE: Giant sequoia in Mariposa Grove. PHOTO © JEFF FOOTT

MARIPOSA GROVE AND WAWONA:

Grove Museum (Galen Clark's cabin) in Upper Grove.   PHOTO © FRED HIRSCHMANN

Majestically towering above their neighbors, the giant sequoias of Mariposa Grove stand supreme—the largest living things in the world. *Sequoiadendron giganteum,* popularly called Big Trees, are often confused with the coast redwood, a cousin species of greater height, but lesser girth. Mariposa Grove consists of a lower and an upper region, altogether containing 481 large trees. Historians aren't sure where credit for the first pioneer sighting of these noble trees belongs. Galen Clark reported that he and Milton Mann, homesteaders in the Wawona area, discovered the Big Trees in 1857, while on a hunting trip a few miles from his Wawona homestead. They had heard rumors of their existence in "big tree stories" told by other hunters.

Clark devoted much of his life to Mariposa Grove. He explored both the lower and upper regions, counted the trees, named the grove for Mariposa County, and concerned himself with their protection. They were eventually included, along with Yosemite Valley, in The Yosemite Grant—legislation signed by President Abraham Lincoln in 1864—which ceded them to the State of California and made them "inalienable for all time."

Mann, anticipating tourist interest in the phenomenal discovery, began to build a trail to the grove. His labor wasn't in vain— the Mariposa Grove of Giant Sequoias soon became a sightseeing "must." Those pioneers who showed an entrepreneurial spirit were not unaware of the profits that could be made by providing beds, meals, and guided tours to what was becoming a steady tourist trade, not only inside Yosemite Valley but along the routes leading to it as well.

Mariposa Grove is situated between 5,500 and 7,000 feet, an elevation range particularly suited to the growth needs of sequoias. In contrast to the bulk of mature trees, their seeds are remarkably tiny—resembling oat flakes—contained in smallish cones about the size of hens' eggs. It takes more than 91,000 seeds to weigh one pound. The seeds are not easily released, requiring the aid of squirrels and insects to eat the cones, dropping the seeds to the ground. The heat from fire may also open the cones. The fibrous, two-foot-thick bark of the sequoia is able to withstand flames, ensuring propagation of the species.

The oldest known sequoia survived for 3,200 years—only the bristlecone pine of eastern California outranks them as the "oldest living things." Some reach a height of nearly 300 feet and measure more than 20 feet in diameter. Sequoias are so immense that even while looking at them it is hard to comprehend how large they really are. News of their discovery was greeted with skepticism. When a cross-section from the base of a sequoia 20 feet thick was cut (from a neighboring grove) and shipped to England, it was dubbed "the Yankee Hoax." To loggers, the wood was a disappointment. After struggling to fall one tree (it took a team of four men 22 days to topple it) the giant fell with a roar and crashed with a shudder. The trunk shattered, and the weak wood ultimately proved to be worthless for construction purposes. Its resistance to decay, however, made it suitable for shingles and fenceposts. This attribute contributes to the sequoias' long life because insects resist invading the tannin-filled bark.

Although the statistics of these trees are impressive and cannot be ignored, it is important to see these trees not only with the mind, but also with the spirit.

J. Smeaton Chase, an Englishman who made two long and leisurely pack-trips in Yosemite, recording his treks in journals, found Mariposa Grove an enchanting place and described his impressions eloquently. He wrote, "As one stands in the dreamlike silence of these groves of ancient trees, the solemnity of their enormous age and size combine to produce a cathedral mood of quietude and receptiveness." He also showed insight and humor, "Lying down at the foot of the pedestal of the Grizzly Giant for an hour, seeing and hearing invisible and inaudible things, a plague on the bloke who blunders into my dream with, 'Half a million feet of lumber in that tree, sir!' Is that all there is to that tree? I assure you, my friend, that I can see vastly more in it if you will but leave me alone."

As I stroll through Mariposa Grove, I enjoy the play of sunlight on the bark of the trunks, shading into variations of reddish brown and gold. Conspicuous is the contrasting black char at the

---

OPPOSITE: South Fork Merced River and historic covered bridge, Wawona. PHOTO © HOWARD WEAMER

Wild azaleas and giant sequoias, Mariposa Grove.

base of many of these sequoias, signs of fires that passed through but didn't destroy. Ahead of me is the Clothespin Tree, with a fire scar burned so far up the trunk that it appears cut in two. The Telescope Tree has been hollowed out by fire—standing inside its base you can look straight up through the crown. Yet, both are healthy trees.

Giant sequoias do not die of old age. After centuries of survival they are eventually felled by storms but continue to lie in state, where we diminutive creatures may approach and marvel at their almost incomprehensible size.

Fire-scarred sequoia trunks, Lower Mariposa Grove.

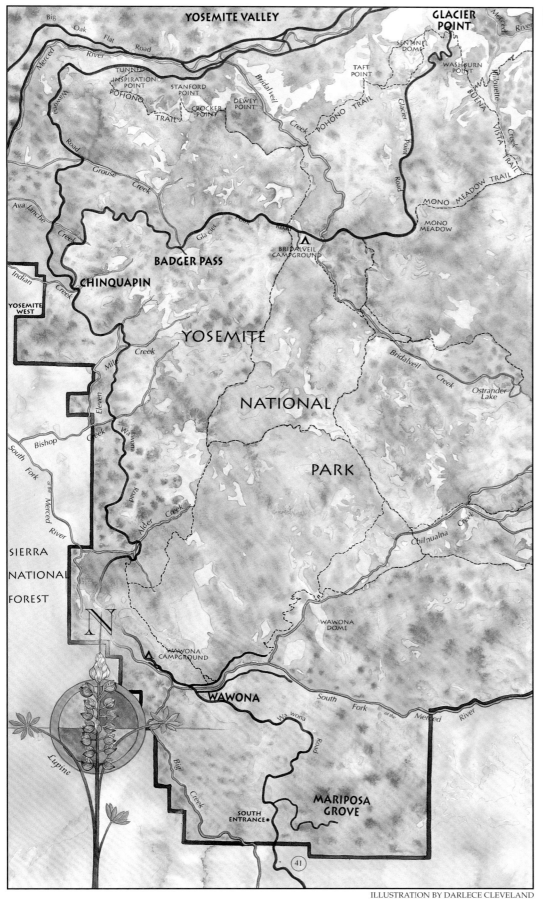

ILLUSTRATION BY DARLECE CLEVELAND

The Wawona area, 30 miles south of Yosemite Valley, is known for its serene atmosphere. Here you will find a park service Information Station, the Wawona Hotel, a campground, stables, and historic Hill's Studio. The Mariposa Grove of Giant Sequoias is only six miles away.

The Wawona area was first settled in 1856, when Galen Clark homesteaded 160 acres. The cabin he built, known as Clark's Station, was a convenient stopping place between Mariposa and Yosemite Valley, and Clark generously provided bed and board, conversation, and mountain lore. He was a good host but a poor businessman who eventually took in a partner, Edwin Moore, in an attempt to recoup losses. However, the recently completed Big Oak Flat and Coulterville Roads, entering Yosemite from the northwest, brought most Yosemite-bound tourists, and Clark and Moore found that they couldn't compete. In December 1874, they sold out to the Washburn brothers. Energetic and enterprising, the Washburns enlarged the lodging area (the site of present-day Wawona Hotel) and began work to complete a stage road to Yosemite Valley. When their road from Mariposa to Yosemite Valley was completed, the Washburn's business began to flourish.

Wawona is the site of the historic Wawona Hotel, built in 1876, during the Washburn's ownership of the area. Galen Clark's cottage, next to the main building, dates back to Clark's original ownership. Historic cabins collected from throughout the park are on display at the Pioneer Yosemite History Center. The bridge Galen Clark built over the South Fork of the Merced River, later "covered" by the Washburns, is now located at the entrance to the history center.

When Yosemite National Park was established in 1890, Yosemite Valley and Mariposa Grove remained under the administration of the State of California. The new park was put under the management of the U.S. Cavalry, with Captain A.E. Wood in charge. Wawona was chosen as the site for park headquarters—now the the Wawona campground. In 1906, when The Yosemite Grant and Yosemite National Park were merged under federal jurisdiction, the army was moved to new headquarters in Yosemite Valley.

Modern conveniences came to Wawona, and elsewhere in Yosemite, in the 20th century and saw expanded hotel facilities, a golf course, and artistic and cultural pursuits. The National Park Service obtained 8,785 acres in the Wawona Basin in 1932, and the stately Victorian-style Wawona Hotel came under management of park concessionaires.

PAGE 44 & 45: The Bachelor and Three Graces, Mariposa Grove. PHOTO © LARRY ULRICH

HUMAN HISTORY

When Major James D. Savage and the Mariposa Battalion came to the clearing, now called Inspiration Point, they looked out on an incredible vista and realized they were near the end of a pursuit. They had a mandate from the Governor of California to find and capture an Indian tribe that was accused of preying on foothill miners and prospectors, and had been told that they made their home in a remarkable hidden valley. Now it lay before them—stupendous cliffs, water falling from a great height, a dome of unique configuration. It was March 1851, a date to be remembered as both a beginning and an ending. Soon European-Americans would initiate a flood of development in this quiet valley, and the relocation of the natives would mark a tragic ending to a lifestyle that had survived for many hundreds of years.

THEY CAME, THEY SAW, THEY STAYED

News of the discovery of the mythical valley quickly spread and the adventurous responded. The seven-square-mile Yosemite Valley was destined to become publicized, populated, cultivated, ravaged, and reconstructed—all within a few decades. The first tourist to arrive was the intrepid James Hutchings who became Yosemite's first publicist. He promoted Yosemite with his book, *Scenes of Wonder and Curiosity*, to which tourists eagerly responded, traveling many days over difficult trails to admire and explore the marvels that he described. Hutchings and other innkeepers soon developed lodgings that were, at first, crude arrangements but which eventually became hotels offering comfortable "bed and board."

An increase in settlement brought questionable changes to the appearance of Yosemite Valley. Settlers sought out the rich valley acreage and sowed its meadows, which flourished with crops of hay for their livestock and soon became criss-crossed with fences. In the high country beyond the valley, herds of sheep followed their appetites, eating their way to higher, greener pastures.

At the Mariposa Grove of Giant Sequoias, Galen Clark, fearing the degradation of these unique groves by an influx of tourists and private interests, used his influence to affect legislation that would ensure the preservation of the "big trees."

THE YOSEMITE GRANT

Fortunately there were visionaries—men who foresaw the eventual destruction of the valley if it were left to those who favored profit over protection. California Senator John Conness submitted a bill to Congress giving Yosemite Valley and the Mariposa Grove of Giant Sequoias to the State of California, to be administered by a Board of Com-

missioners. President Lincoln signed the act that established The Yosemite Grant in 1864, the first legal affirmation of an unprecedented idea: setting aside a public landscape for the enjoyment of the people.

The Yosemite Grant was a milestone piece of legislation, but it was not enough. Galen Clark was appointed Guardian of Yosemite, a position created under the provisions of the Grant. He soon saw that even greater government protection was needed. A man devoted to both Yosemite Valley and Mariposa Grove, Clark acted on his preservationist principles to the extent that he could, but the responsibilities taxed his time and energy. Along with other protectionists, he saw the need for more widespread governmental regulation.

THE CREATION OF YOSEMITE NATIONAL PARK

John Muir arrived in Yosemite Valley four years after The Yosemite Grant had been enacted, a footloose young man with a passion for Nature, who discovered in Yosemite a spiritual home. During his first Sierra summer he took a job as overseer for a shepherd and his flock in the Sierra high country, and saw the devastation caused by what he would later label "hoofed locusts." Aware of the lack of regulation over this type of destruction, Muir became a champion for the preservation of all of Yosemite's natural resources. He was convinced, as was Galen Clark, that government protection needed to be extended to land surrounding Yosemite Valley. With his friend and ally, influential *Century* magazine publisher Robert Underwood Johnson, he de-

ABOVE: Troop F, Sixth Cavalry, on The Fallen Monarch, Mariposa Grove, 1899. PHOTO COURTESY NPS, YOSEMITE COLLECTION

veloped plans for a national park, an idea that received support throughout the country. As a result of their efforts, Yosemite would become a national park on October 1, 1890.

Now there were two Yosemites—plus a Mariposa Grove. In 1891, the U.S. Cavalry was brought in to supervise Yosemite National Park, under the innovative direction of Captain Abram Wood. Wood dealt with illegal grazing of sheep by charging herders with the only legal charge under his jurisdiction, trespassing, then ejecting them at opposite corners of the park from their flocks. The untended sheep were scattered or eaten by predators. The cavalry also constructed trails, surveyed boundaries, mapped the park in detail, and stocked lakes with trout. Although the cavalry effectively handled the lands known as Yosemite National Park, the management difficulty of the confusing geography between the park and The Yosemite Grant became obvious. Through the efforts of the Sierra Club—which Muir had been instrumental in founding—and with the help of President Teddy Roosevelt, whose support Muir encouraged during their historic campfire talks, California receded the Grant properties to the federal government in 1905. The Cavalry withdrew when war began in Europe and, in 1916, the National Park Service came into being.

MODERN TIMES

Under the National Park Service, Yosemite moved into the modern age and many welcome changes came quickly. But some asked, "Was the park improved by development?" How could one improve on Half Dome, El Capitan, and Yosemite Falls? The automobile, at first a curiosity, became a contentious

subject of debate. Automobiles increased visitation and park management looked at the numbers and was pleased—more visitors proved that the National Park idea was a success. Today, many believe Yosemite is being glutted by this success. Visitation topped 3 million in 1999, putting a strain on both natural and human resources. During the past decade, many management plans have

been proposed, but none have been able to satisfy opposing factions who express strong feelings about Yosemite's future. An ongoing debate brews over where to draw the line between preservation and use. How to reconcile the protection of Yosemite with the demands of the public is a conundrum to which there appears to be no immediate solution.

THE AWAHNICHI

Native Americans have occupied Yosemite Valley for at least 4,000 years and perhaps—as suggested by archeological findings—as many as 8,000 to 10,000 years. The natives sought by the Mariposa Battalion, in 1851, were descendants of Southern Sierra Miwoks. They called their valley *awahni*, "place of the gaping mouth," referring to the valley's depth and shape, thus they came to be known as *awahnichi*. Miwok residents west of Yosemite sometimes referred to valley natives as *yohemite* or *yohometuk,* which translates to "some of them are killers." Because the Mariposa Battalion was familiar with the word *yohemite*, they thought it appropriate to give the valley the name of its residents. Eventual variations in sound and spelling created "Yosemite."

The *awahnichi* occupied Yosemite Valley mostly during the warm seasons of the year. During winter, some moved to the foothills, others traveled to the eastern side of the Sierra to trade with the Paiutes at Mono Lake, bringing fern root, manzanita berries, and acorns—returning with obsidian, pine nuts, and *ki-cha-vee*, an insect larvae delicacy. As hunters and gatherers, they made extensive use of the valley's resources, but acorns from the black oak were their dietary staple. They perfected techniques of preparation—hulling, grinding, and leaching out bitter tannins—before boiling the meal in water-filled baskets heated with hot stones. The women excelled at making baskets of all shapes and sizes featuring intricate designs, prized today by collectors. The California Gold Rush of 1849, and the subsequent military discovery of Yosemite Valley, brought an irrevocable end to the lifestyle of the *awahnichi*.

ABOVE: Mono-Paiute woman near Yosemite Falls. PHOTO COURTESY NPS, YOSEMITE COLLECTION

El Capitan and Yosemite Valley seen from Taft Point, late afternoon.

GLACIER POINT ROAD

A visit to Glacier Point, a magnificent overlook on the tip of Yosemite Valley's south rim, is considered a highlight of touring Yosemite National Park during those months when Glacier Point Road is open. The road is closed following the first major snowstorm of winter, usually reopening by late-May. The view from Glacier Point elicits the words "breathtaking" and "awesome" to describe the astounding panorama. Not only does Glacier Point command a full view of the High Sierra crest—peak after peak in full array—but from the railed platform you look straight down into Yosemite Valley, 3,200 feet below.

Directly east is Half Dome, from this vantage a more personal view than from the floor of Yosemite Valley. To the right, south of Half Dome, you see two of Yosemite's most famous waterfalls, Nevada and Vernal, the "staircase" falls of the Merced Canyon. Their size is diminished when seen from this height, but at maximum flow their roar can be heard distinctly. Glacier Point rises directly behind Curry Village, its sheer vertical face making possible the famous Firefall, discontinued since 1968. Embers pushed over the brink fell in one uninterrupted descent, creating the effect of a waterfall of fire.

Hiking trails accessed from Glacier Point Road include the Panorama Trail (to the top of Nevada Fall) and the Mono Meadow, Taft Point, McGurk Meadow, and Sentinel Dome Trails. The Four-Mile Trail from Yosemite Valley to Glacier Point is actually about 5 miles long since the trail has been re-routed and extended. A tour bus from Yosemite Valley transports hikers to Glacier Point for a charge, and they can then hike down to the valley floor. Inquire at the Yosemite Lodge Tour Desk for a bus schedule.

Activities occurring here in summer and early fall include ranger walks to Taft Point, photography walks, sunset talks, the spectacle of a full moon rising, and "Stars-over-Yosemite" astronomy talks. See *The Yosemite Guide* for a listing of dates, times, and meeting places.

To reach Glacier Point, take Wawona Road (Highway 41) to Chinquapin Junction and turn east onto Glacier Point Road. Glacier Point is 16 miles from the junction. The road is closed to vehicles beyond Badger Pass Ski Area in winter, but the snow-packed road is groomed for cross-country skiers who may arrange to spend the night at the chalet at Glacier Point.

OPPOSITE: Summer thunderstorm above Half Dome seen from Glacier Point. PHOTO © MICHAEL FRYE

INTO THE WILDERNESS:

Sierra crest from Cathedral Peak, sunset.   PHOTO © GALEN ROWELL/MOUNTAIN LIGHT

A trip into Yosemite's wilderness has been mythologized by lovers of wildness as the ultimate escape, characterized by an absence of what are generally termed "the trappings of civilization." Jayne Kestler, an experienced backpacker, describes how it feels to get away from what she calls human stuff, "Everything slows down once you are miles away from roads. You have your boots and your pack, you're self-contained, you have found freedom. There's no other feeling like it." Jayne never fails to find fulfillment while exploring Yosemite's wilderness areas. She has hiked all 800 miles of Yosemite's maintained trails, plus an additional 200 miles cross-country. "Everyone who goes into the wilderness has a personal reason," she explains, "Some go for the views. I go for the kinesthetics—the touch. Gravel underfoot, reaching out to boulders, sleeping on a granite dome. That's how I connect with the energy of the universe."

Visitors to Yosemite's wilderness enjoy its diversity, including a range of elevations that culminate in 13,000-foot peaks along the Sierra crest. In the heart of these mountains the remnants of glaciers that carved Yosemite's topography can still be seen and the geologic effects of glacial action are evident everywhere—most notably in the abundance of lakes found in the High Sierra. The Sierra has been labeled "the gentle wilderness"—a phrase with several meanings. It can refer to the favorable weather conditions generally experienced during the Sierran summer. Temperatures are almost never extreme and summer days tend to be dry and sunny. "Gentle" has a deeper implication for Jayne. "Yosemite shares itself with you," is the way she puts it. "Unlike other areas of the Sierra, such as Desolation Wilderness or Mineral King, Yosemite's wilderness offers gentle diversions. A forest trail tangled with downed trees will open up to welcoming meadows. After hours of difficulty struggling up and down, then up again in a series of canyons, you're rewarded with jewel-like lakes, waiting with their embrace of silver coolness."

Ninety-four percent of Yosemite is now designated "wilderness" and is managed in a manner that guarantees the preservation of its natural conditions. The Wilderness District staff, under the Division of Visitor Protection, includes wilderness rangers assigned to oversee the entire region, monitoring conditions created by Mother Nature as well as caused by park visitors. Issuing and monitoring Wilderness Permits is a key responsibility. Permission was not always needed to enter Yosemite's wilderness, but when backpacking became popular, in the early 1970s, Yosemite's most frequented destinations became threatened by overuse. Requiring Wilderness Permits limits the number of people allowed access from trailheads, is a way to educate users about personal safety and protection of the environment, and reduces human impact on trails and campsites.

A decision to measure human impact on the wilderness resulted in a three-part field study, conducted in the 1970s, 80s, and mid-90s. Significant wilderness management decisions were based on changes that were found to have occurred over this 30-year period.

For the mid-80s study, conducted over four summers (one season for each of Yosemite's four topographic quadrangles) Jayne and I were one of two teams assigned to monitor Yosemite's northwest quad. Using maps, tools, and guidelines we learned to precisely measure certain aspects of trails and campsites. These measurements included the depth of ruts in sections of abused trails, the number and size of campsites created by backpackers (including new campfire rings built in preference to existing rings of stones), impacts on campsite ground-cover, and the addition of "conveniences" to campsites—such as nails driven into trees.

The first season was a trial run and the study was redesigned and completed four years later. Although I only worked for one summer, it proved to be a revelation of what wilderness can give and what can be learned from it. My previous Sierra experiences had been more or less follow-the-leader outings that called for enthusiasm and broken-in boots. My months with the Wilderness Study were not filled with days of simply monitoring trail miles interspersed by routine tasks. The wilderness demanded something from me—and gave in return. Every day brought insights concerning the landscape and I was tested in meaningful, and

Mount Ansel Adams and Lyell Fork of the Merced River, sunset.

sometimes seemingly trivial, ways. The trivial: fighting echelons of mosquitoes and, one unforgettable afternoon, an attack of ants that ravaged our packs and almost destroyed our equanimity. The personal meaning of this experience, my first wholehearted encounter with Yosemite's wilderness, is too emotionally complicated to express. It is enough to say that I discovered two of the wilderness' unmatchable gifts, solitude and spiritual renewal, plus an inexplicable sense of "coming home."

Le Conte Falls, Grand Canyon of the Tuolumne River.

Upper McCabe Lake in its glacially scoured basin.

PHOTO © GEORGE WUERTHNER

Hiking is a major pastime of Yosemite visitors. The setting couldn't be more inspiring—destinations are plentiful, the weather cooperative, and the possibilities for finding a trail suited to one's stamina and experience are excellent. Day hikes are the most sought after outdoor pastime by visitors who have no more than a few days, or hours, to get close to the scenery. "Hike" is usually defined as footwork involving distance and expended energy, but for day-trippers in Yosemite the concept of a "hike" seems to be related to one's expectations. A family at the Valley Visitor Center wants a "short, flat hike that our children can enjoy"—the recommendation is Happy Isles: flat paths, creeks in season, and a Nature Center. A man admitting to being out of condition asks about "an easy hike, possibly near a meadow"—the recommendation: a portion of the Valley Loop Trail. Innocent confidence is reflected in the eyes of two robust boys who ask, "Will it take more than a couple of hours to hike to the top of Half Dome?" They are told this is a 17-mile round-trip trek rated "very strenuous."

In every area of Yosemite you can find a day hike to your liking. Trails are rated easy, moderate, or strenuous. "Easy" typically means a walk along a flat road or a gently sloping path, perhaps including some rolling terrain. You can expect most destinations out of Yosemite Valley to require at least some uphill exertion—such as Vernal Fall, Nevada Fall, and Upper Yosemite Fall. The walk to the base of Lower Yosemite Fall, on the other hand, is a 20-minute stroll. In Tuolumne Meadows, the walk from Lembert Dome to Parsons Lodge via Soda Springs (two miles round-trip) is also easy, and affords vistas of Unicorn and Cathedral Peaks. For spectacular views, achieved with minimum effort, choose the Taft Point Trail—a one-mile walk through the forest that brings you to the edge of Yosemite Valley's south rim. The trailhead is accessed from Glacier Point Road. In the Hetchy Hetchy area, the trail to Wapama Falls is considered moderate (five miles round-trip) on a well-maintained, easy to follow path.

An excellent selection of maps and guidebooks is available at visitor centers, where free day-hike information sheets for Yosemite Valley, Wawona, Glacier Point, Hetch Hetchy, and Tuolumne Meadows are also available.

WILDFLOWERS

Stonecrop, Merced River Canyon. PHOTO © JEFF GRANDY

Showy milkweed. PHOTO © JIM WILSON

Snow plant. PHOTO © JIM WILSON

Yosemite's wildflowers are eagerly anticipated, identified, photographed, and enjoyed by botany enthusiasts. However, be forewarned: you may seek and not find unless you remember the wildflower season in Yosemite is not related to the calendar, but to elevation. "Spring" creeps slowly, but surely, up the mountain bringing plants out of dormancy and into their complex preparations for the production of fruits and seeds. The most heralded part of this process is the flowering.

Yosemite's wildflower season begins with buttercups in the foothills in early March. The succession of blossoming proceeds to increasingly higher elevations through the months that follow. Flower-finding is best done on foot along roadsides, in shaded woodlands, and in open meadows. The season ends with brief displays on upland plateaus. Some hardy plants, such as monkeyflower, flourish from the foothills to above timberline.

April in Yosemite Valley brings a gradual greening, but valley meadows are too moist for much of a wildflower show, although they do support western azalea (a flowering shrub) and cow parsnip. Mountain violets and bleeding hearts can be found in the valley's woodsy habitats. The drier meadows of summer favor sneezeweed and the tall stalks of showy milkweed. Appearing in August, *lessingia*—a rayless aster—colors meadows blue and purple well into October. Fall color is also supplied by meadow goldenrod.

By early July, elephant's head and shooting stars begin blooming in the meadows of Crane Flat. At 6,000 feet, these boggy places also appeal to the Sierra rein orchid, one of a dozen members of the orchid family found in the park. The Pohono Trail, along Yosemite Valley's south rim, offers 13 miles of wildflower discovery: red columbine, meadow rue, purple monkshood, lupine, senecio, leopard lily, and pinedrops. The blood-red stalks of snow plant light up the duff of the forest floor.

Along Tioga Road, mountain pride is more than eye-catching—its hot-pink petals glow against the granite backdrop. Flowering is delayed until July in Tuolumne Meadows, a sub-alpine zone at an elevation of 8,600 feet. Conspicuous by mid-summer are Lemmon's paintbrush, aster (mountain daisy), deer's tongue, pussypaws, dwarf shooting star, and whorled penstemon. Late in August, purple gentians push through drying grasses, but they are not the year's finale. At treeline and above plants are smaller and there are fewer days in bloom, but there is an unexpectedly diverse selection, including *Lewisia*, alpine gold, draba, columbine, lupine, and dwarf paintbrush.

Bleeding hearts. PHOTO © JEFF GRANDY

Heather and laurel. PHOTO © JIM WILSON

Lemmons paintbrush. PHOTO © MICHAEL FRYE

Western redbud (shrub form).   PHOTO © MICHAEL FRYE

Ponderosa pine.   PHOTO © CARR CLIFTON

Pacific dogwood.   PHOTO © JEFF D. NICHOLAS

Splendid trees dominate Yosemite's varied plant communities. *Conifers,* cone-bearing trees with needles, and *deciduous* trees, which drop their leaves every year, are both abundant in the park, the latter primarily in Yosemite Valley. A visitor unfamiliar with mountain vegetation may only see a landscape of similar looking "evergreens," but various species soon become distinct. Observers should note a tree's height, girth, bark, contour, leaf shape, cones, and needle clusters.

A key to identifying Yosemite's trees, especially the conifers, is to note at what elevation you find them. As John Muir remarked, "The traveler will never be at a loss in determining his elevation above sea-level by watching the trees, inasmuch as they take on new forms corresponding to variations in altitude."

Exactly half of the 18 conifers found in Yosemite are pines. In order, from lower to higher elevations, these are the ponderosa, or yellow, pine—many in Yosemite Valley—look for trunks up to six feet in diameter, needles grouped in 3's, and a jig-saw-puzzle look to the yellowish bark. The sugar pine is known for its straight, purplish-barked bole, and 15- to 18-inch cones—astounding to early explorers and startling even today. The Jeffrey pine grows at higher elevations (typical locale: Glacier Point) and is similar to the ponderosa, but "prickly ponderosa" cones have sharp points while "gentle Jeffrey" cones are easily handled. Jeffrey pine bark is fragrant—some compare it to vanilla or pineapple. The large and long-lived Douglas fir shares this "pine belt" along with the white fir. Incense cedar is also found at this elevation, populating slopes up to about 5,000 feet, its deeply grooved reddish bark as distinctive as its sweeping, flat, fragrant boughs. Pines growing at higher elevations include the lodgepole (needles in 2's), and the whitebark (needles in 5's). The magnificent red fir dominates the upper forests; its range is broad, between 6,000 and 9,000 feet.

Of Yosemite's *deciduous* trees, the canyon live oak is scattered throughout Yosemite Valley, as is the California black oak—which is distinguished by its size (sometimes topping 75 feet) and, in autumn, by its rich gold leaves. The Pacific dogwood's distinctive whitish-green "petals" (actually bracts, the center is a cluster of flowers) are a welcome sign of spring. Streamsides and riverbanks are home to graceful willows, white alders, and balsam-scented cottonwoods.

Big-leaf maple.   PHOTO © JEFF D. NICHOLAS

Western juniper.   PHOTO © JEFF GNASS

Black oak.   PHOTO © CARR CLIFTON

MAMMALS

Mule deer buck. PHOTO © MICHAEL FRYE

Bobcat. PHOTO © MICHAEL FRYE

Yellow-bellied marmot. PHOTO © MICHAEL FRYE

When Yosemite visitors ask, "Where can I see wildlife?" they hope to see the unusual, yet most of the more than 75 species of mammals in the Yosemite area are rarely seen by humans—primarily because their habitats are not near "people places." On the other hand, small mammals—such as squirrels and chipmunks—are often observed darting about near dwellings and campgrounds.

At least five chipmunk species are found in the park. They are distinguished by their coloration (reddish brown with black-and-white striped backs) and are smaller than squirrels. The most common squirrel in Yosemite Valley is the California ground squirrel, but the following species are also present: the western gray squirrel (bushy tail), the Sierra chickaree (known for its high-pitched squeak), and the Belding ground squirrel. The golden-manteled ground squirrel resembles a chipmunk, but its side stripes stop at its shoulders, while a chipmunk's

stripes continue to its nose. Higher elevations are home to Belding ground squirrels, familiarly known as "picket pins" because of their habit of standing erect and motionless when it senses danger.

Mule deer, named for their large mule-like ears, are common at elevations between 3,500 and 8,500 feet. They can be seen browsing in the meadows of Yosemite Valley and Wawona, oblivious to being watched or photographed. Deer may appear tame, having been exposed to humans for many years without feeling threatened, but they can react unpredictably by using their sharp hooves and antlers.

The black bear is the largest mammal found in the park. It can be brown or cinnamon-colored, as well as black. Wary visitors often confuse it with the grizzly bear, which has not been seen in Yosemite since 1895.

Coyotes are commonly noticed trotting along valley roads or hunting in meadows

during winter—their gray fur and dark tail conspicuous against the snow. Visitors often mistake coyotes for wolves, but wolves are much larger and are no longer part of Yosemite's ecosystem.

Yellow-bellied marmots are frequently seen at Olmsted Point, on Tioga Road, darting around boulders and rock piles, sounding their characteristic whistle. Badgers exist in the park, but tend to be elusive, as are pine martens, ringtails, porcupines, bobcats, and weasels. Bighorn sheep were released in the Tioga Pass area in 1986, in hopes of re-establishing them in Yosemite. Watch for them on high rocky promontories above the road.

Black bear. PHOTO © JEFF FOOTT

Gray squirrel in ponderosa pine. PHOTO © MICHAEL FRYE

Howling coyotes. PHOTO © MICHAEL FRYE

American dipper (water ouzel).   PHOTO © MICHAEL FRYE

Mountain bluebird.   PHOTO © DIANA STRATTON

Red-winged blackbird.   PHOTO © MICHAEL FRYE

Yosemite is one of California's premier birding destinations. Its diverse habitats (open, dry woodlands, dense coniferous forests, riparian thickets, shrubby hillsides, alpine meadows, and talus slopes) encompass an elevation range from rolling foothills at 2,000 feet to 14,000-foot windswept peaks. With the widely varying seasonal changes that accompany such differences in elevation, it is no surprise that Yosemite's more than 240 species of birds are mostly seasonal migrants. Many visitors are surprised to discover how many birds they recognize even within the space of a short visit. Quickly identified are colorful robins, noisy Stellar's jays and black-and-white Clark's nutcrackers, acorn woodpeckers (black and white body and red cap), and Western tanagers (bright yellow body with an orange-red head).

Other valley birds that might be seen on a walk, or from a quiet spot at the edge of a meadow, are the winter wren, dark-eyed junco, band-tailed pigeon, flicker, oriole, nuthatch, chickadee, and sparrow. When near the Merced River look for belted kingfishers swooping close to the water's surface to feed on fish. At higher elevations, such as Tuolumne Meadows, you might see a rock wren, pine grosbeak (the largest grosbeak in North America), white-crowned sparrow, or mountain bluebird.

The only known active peregrine falcon nests, or eyries, in the entire Sierra Nevada are found in Yosemite—peregrines were found to be breeding at an El Capitan site in 1978. The story of the successful "hands-on-management" of this endangered species has brought widespread attention. When it was discovered that the peregrine's reproductive cycle was being interrupted by egg-breakage caused by the incubating female—the result of "eggshell thinning" from the birds' ingestion of DDT—the park service began collaborating with the Santa Cruz Predatory Bird Research Group. In an innovative procedure, thin-shelled natural eggs were removed from the nest and hatched in a laboratory incubator. Artificial eggs were then substituted for the fragile eggs that had been removed from the nest. In time, these were replaced with newly hatched nestlings from the laboratory. The captive-hatched young are subsequently fledged (raised to independence) by adult falcons. This removal and replacement of eggs and hatchlings has been accomplished by skilled rock climbers. Ideally, natural processes should not be interfered with, but the park's goal is to restore natural conditions—to the fullest extent feasible—that can then be maintained by allowing natural processes to operate largely unimpaired.

Great gray owl.   PHOTO © MICHAEL FRYE

Steller's jay.   PHOTO © MICHAEL FRYE

Peregrine falcon.   PHOTO © JEFF VANUGA

PAGE 60 & 61: Upper Yosemite Fall, spring flow. PHOTO © TOM TILL

RESOURCES & INFORMATION

EMERGENCY & MEDICAL:
24-HOUR EMERGENCY MEDICAL SERVICE
Dial 911 *(From hotel rooms dial 9-911)*

YOSEMITE MEDICAL CLINIC
(209) 372-4637

EMERGENCY ROAD SERVICE
(209) 372-8320

ROAD CONDITIONS:
ROAD & WEATHER	(209) 372-0200 (24 *hr*)
CAL TRANS	(800) 427-7623
NEVADA	(702) 486-3116

FOR MORE INFORMATION:
NATIONAL PARKS ON THE INTERNET:
www.nps.gov

YOSEMITE NATIONAL PARK
PO Box 577
Yosemite, CA 95389
(209) 372-0200, TTD (209) 372-4726,
TTY (209) 372-0265, (209) 372-0265 *(Public Information)*
www.nps.gov/yose/

YOSEMITE ASSOCIATION
PO Box 230
EL PORTAL, CA 95318
www.yosemite.org

YOSEMITE INSTITUTE
(209) 379-9511
www.yni.org

PACK TRIPS
(559) 253-5674

YOSEMITE MOUNTAINEERING SCHOOL
(209) 372-8344

WILDERNESS PERMITS
(209) 372-0740

BADGER PASS SKI AREA
(209) 372-8430

LODGING INSIDE THE PARK:
YOSEMITE CONCESSION SERVICES
(559) 252-4848
www.yosemitepark.com

CAMPING INSIDE THE PARK:
YOSEMITE CONCESSION SERVICES
(800) 436-PARK, TDD (888)530-9796
International (301) 722-1257
www.yosemitepark.com

LODGING OUTSIDE THE PARK:
MARIPOSA COUNTY VISITORS BUREAU
Mariposa, CA 95338
(888) 554-9012
www.mariposa.org

MAMMOTH VISITOR CENTER
Mammoth Lakes, CA 93546
(760) 924-5500
www.r5.fs.fed.us/inyo

TUOLUMNE COUNTY VISITORS CENTER
Sonora, CA 95370
(800) 446-1333
www.thegreatunfenced.com

YOSEMITE SIERRA VISITORS BUREAU
Oakhurst, CA 93644
(559) 683-4636
www.yosemite-sierra.org

CAMPING OUTSIDE THE PARK:
INYO NATIONAL FOREST
Bishop, CA 93514
(760) 873-2400
www.r5.fs.fed.us/inyo

MONO BASIN NATIONAL FOREST SCENIC AREA
Lee Vinning, CA 93541
www.r5.fs.fed.us/inyo

SIERRA NATIONAL FOREST
Clovis, CA 93612
(559) 297-0706
www.r5.fs.fed.us/sierra

STANISLAUS NATIONAL FOREST
Sonora, CA 95370
(209) 532-3671
www.r5.fs.fed.us/stanislaus

TOIYABE NATIONAL FOREST
Sparks, NV 89431
(775) 355-5302
www.gorp.com/gorp/resource/us_national_forest/
nv_toiya

OTHER REGIONAL SITES:
BODIE STATE PARK
Bridgeport, CA 93517
(760) 647-6445
www.ceres.ca.gov/sierradsp/bodie/htmo

CALIFORNIA STATE MINING &
MINERAL MUSEUM
Mariposa, CA 95338
email: mineralmuseum@sierratel.com

CALAVERAS BIG TREES STATE PARK
Murphys, CA
(209) 795-2334
www.sierra.parks.state.ca.usa/cbt/btfacts.htm

COLUMBIA STATE HISTORIC PARK
Columbia, CA 95310
(209) 532-0150
www.sierra.parks.state.ca.us

DEATH VALLEY NATIONAL PARK
Death Valley, CA 92328-059
(760) 786-2331
www.nps,gov/deva

DEVILS POSTPILE NATIONAL MONUMENT
c/o Sequoia & Kings Canyon National Parks
Three Rivers, CA 93271

MANZANAR NATIONAL HISTORIC SITE
Independence, CA 93526-0426
(760) 878-2932
www.nps.gov/manz

RAILTOWN 1897 STATE HISTORIC PARK
Jamestown, CA 95327
(209) 984-3953
www.csrmf.org

SEQUOIA/KINGS CANYON NATIONAL PARK
Three Rivers, CA 93271-9651
(559) 565-3341
www.nps.gov/seki

SUGGESTED READING:
Arno, Stephen F. *DISCOVERING SIERRA TREES*, NPS, Yosemite Association, 1973.

Bunnell, Dr. Layfayette, *DISCOVERY OF THE YOSEMITE IN 1851*. Outdoor Books,, Olympic Valley, California, 1977.

Gaines, David. *BIRDS OF YOSEMITE AND THE EAST SLOPE*. Artemis Press, Lee Vining, CA, 1988

Grater, Russell K. *DISCOVERING SIERRA MAMMALS*, NPS, Yosemite Association, 1978

Johnston, Hank. *THE YOSEMITE GRANT*, 1864-1906. Yosemite Association, YIP, 1995

Matthes, Francois E., *THE INCOMPARABLE VALLEY: AN ECOLOGIC INTERPRETATION OF THE YOSEMITE*. Berkeley: University of California, 1956.

Medley, Steven. *THE COMPLETE GUIDEBOOK TO YOSEMITE NATIONAL PARK*. The Yosemite Association, 1999.

Muir, John. *THE YOSEMITE*. Doubleday-Anchor (reprint, the Century Co.) New York, 1962

Runte, Alfred. 1990. *YOSEMITE: THE EMBATTLED WILDERNESS*. University of Nebraska Press, Lincoln, Nebraska,1990

Russell, Carl P. *100 YEARS IN YOSEMITE*. Yosemite National Park: Yosemite Association, 1978

Sargent, Shirley, *YOSEMITE'S HISTORIC WAWONA*. Flying Spur Press, Foresta, CA, 1975

Schaeffer, Jeffrey. *YOSEMITE NATIONAL PARK*. The Wilderness Press, Berkeley, California, 1999.

Storer, Tracy, and Robert Usinger. 1963. *SIERRA NEVADA NATURAL HISTORY: AN ILLUSTRATED HANDBOOK*. Berkeley: University of California Press.

Wilson, Lynn & Wilson, Jim & Nicholas, Jeff. (1987). Reprint. *WILDFLOWERS OF YOSEMITE*. Mariposa, CA: Sierra Press, Inc. 1992.

OPPOSITE: Sierra juniper and lunar eclipse (time-lapse sequence). PHOTO © MICHAEL FRYE

ACKNOWLEDGMENTS:

I would like to extend a special thanks to National Park Service employees Rick Smith (Chief of Interpretation), Bob Fry, Ginger Burley, Laura Boyers, Jim Snyder, Dean Shenk, Kate McCurdy, Shelton Johnson, Steve Thompson, Norma Craig, Barbara Baroza, and Linda Eade for their invaluable assistance in the production of this title. As always, a very special thanks to all the photographers who shared their personal visions of Yosemite with us during the editing of this title. To all, my profound and sincere thanks!—JDN

PRODUCTION CREDITS:

Author: Ardeth Huntington
Book Design: Jeff D. Nicholas
Photo Editors: Jeff D. Nicholas and
            Marcia Huskey
Illustrations: Darlece Cleveland
Illustrations Graphics: Marcia Huskey
Printing Coordination: Sung In Printing
            America, Inc.

ISBN 1-58071-035-2 (Paper)
ISBN 1-58071-036-0 (Cloth)
COPYRIGHT 2001 BY:
Panorama International Productions, Inc.
4988 Gold Leaf Drive
Mariposa, CA 95338

Sierra Press is an imprint of
Panorama International Productions, Inc.

SIERRA PRESS

4988 Gold Leaf Drive
Mariposa, CA 95338
(209) 966-5071, (209) 966-5073 (Fax)
e-mail: siepress@sti.net

Visit our Website at:
www.NationalParksUSA.com

SIERRA PRESS

OPPOSITE:
Half Dome, mid-winter sunset.
PHOTO © JEFF NICHOLAS